THE LAKES

PHOTOGRAPHS OF THE LAKE DISTRICT
COLIN BAXTER

'87.

First published in Great Britain in 1987 by
Colin Baxter Photography Ltd.,
Lamington, Biggar, Lanarkshire, ML12 6HW
Copyright © Colin Baxter, 1987
All rights reserved

British Library Cataloguing in Publication Data

Baxter, Colin
The Lakes: photographs of the Lake District
1. Lake District (England)—Description
and travel—Views
I. Title
942.7'80858'0222   DA670.L1

ISBN 0-948661-99-2

**The text for The Lakes was researched
and written by Alan Edwards**

**Cover, design and concept by
Charles Miller Graphics, Edinburgh.**

**Printed and produced by Frank Peters
Printers Ltd., Kendal, Cumbria.**

Assembly Pauline Thorburn
Calligraphy Oisín E. J. Peters
Typeset by Image Services Ltd., Edinburgh
Colour Separations by Reprogen Ltd., Leeds
Bound by Hunter & Foulis Ltd., Edinburgh

THE LAKES

PHOTOGRAPHS OF THE LAKE DISTRICT
COLIN BAXTER

COLIN BAXTER PHOTOGRAPHY LTD., LAMINGTON

Contents

Ullswater *opposite page*

BIOGRAPHICAL NOTE

Colin Baxter was born in 1954. He studied photography in Edinburgh from 1978-81, and now lives in rural Lanarkshire. His work has become well-known through exhibitions, books, and postcards—with collections of cards covering The Lake District, Yorkshire, The Scottish Highlands, and elsewhere. His previous books are 'Scotland—The Light and the Land' (1985), 'Colin Baxter's Edinburgh' (1986), and, most recently, a series of booklets entitled 'Experience Scotland'.

Those who only know of the Lake District by reputation are often surprised to find that it covers a relatively small area—about forty miles across. Nevertheless, what it lacks in size it more than makes up for in diversity of scenery. The landscape that was formed here in geological times was one of extremes, the like of which can be found nowhere else in England.

THE LAND OF LAKES AND MOUNTAINS

The rugged mountains, the green valleys and tree-lined lakes, the woods carpeted with wild flowers, the clear streams and the towering waterfalls, all combine to give the region its unique place at the heart of scenic England. And, in a way, the very compactness of the Lake District has added to its charm. A single day's walk can take the visitor through such a variety of unspoilt countryside, from breathtaking mountain vistas to peaceful wooded glades, that the experience is always new and rewarding.

Yet for centuries these splendours went virtually unnoticed. Cumbria was a remote corner of the country, of little economic importance, and peopled by close-knit, independent, communities whose language and customs bore little resemblance to those of their southern neighbours. As the geography of the area suggests, they had more in common with the Scots and Welsh than with the English. For many years the fell farmers of Cumbria struggled to eke a living from the land in much the same way as their Celtic counterparts elsewhere.

Indeed the history of the Lake District is woven around this struggle to tame the land; to bring it, bit by bit, under man's control. Here and there he has succeeded, but the spectacular beauties of the region have survived intact. Even today, in many remote places, man's presence seems no more than a scribbled signature on a vast canvas.

Windermere, Swirl
How and Wetherlam

Thirlmere and Lonscale Fell

Soulby Fell near Ullswater

Above the Vale of Keswick, in the shadow of Skiddaw, stands the Castlerigg stone circle. It was built some five thousand years ago and, like similar circles at Little Salkeld and Swinside, it serves as a reminder of early man's presence in this wild and beautiful landscape. The exact purpose of these megalithic circles is wrapped in mystery but we do know that they were constructed by tribes whose ancestors had arrived many centuries before.

CIRCLES OF STONE

The earliest settlers probably travelled overland from the Baltic regions not long after the last Ice Age, at a time before the North Sea was formed. These Stone Age men led a nomadic life, mainly confined to the coast where fish and game were plentiful and flint was available for their tools.

Later a second, more advanced, group arrived. They came, via Ireland, from the eastern Mediterranean and were skilled in the herding of animals, pottery, and weaving. Moving inland they established the first settlements in the interior of Cumbria and, using their polished stone axes, made the first assaults on the dense forests. An axe factory at Stake Pass, near Great Langdale, tells of their presence and their industry.

Little is known of the Iron Age period which followed the era of the stone circles—although hill forts at Castle Crag, Borrowdale and Carrock Fell probably date from that time. They may have been built by tribes known as the Brigantes who had entered the region from the east. The Romans, who arrived in northern England in AD 79, set about destroying these primitive fortifications.

Seathwaite, Dunnerdale, and the sea, from Bow Fell

Lake Windermere and Wray Castle

Watendlath Tarn and Bleatarn Gill

Langdale Pikes and Windermere

Preston Patrick, near Kendal

To the Romans Cumbria was useful only in forming a line of communication for their advance into Scotland. Consequently the signs of their presence are military ones—roads, forts, barracks—with no trace of the villas or temples normally associated with Roman occupation. Welsh was the language of the Celtic tribes when the Romans arrived in the north and it remained so when, in the fourth century, they finally left. In fact Welsh was spoken in Cumbria almost until the time of the Norman Conquest.

The Romans built a road through the high fells from Watercrook, near Kendal, to the coast at Ravenglass, along which they established a series of forts. Extensive remains of one of these can be found at Waterhead, near Ambleside; and Hardknott Fort, positioned high above the Esk Valley, ranks as one of the most spectacular sites.

THE ROMANS

Yet while the Romans left little evidence of their civilising power, the presence of their garrisons almost certainly brought a stability to the area. When Hadrian's Wall was finally evacuated the Scots and Picts were quick to come south, devastating many of Cumbria's coastal settlements and depriving the tribes of their richest lands. Once again poverty and barbarism became features of Cumbrian life.

Hardknott Fort, Goat Crag and Whin Rigg

Latterbarrow and Windermere
Windermere from near Troutbeck *previous page*

Rayrigg Wyke, Windermere

The Dark Ages which followed the departure of the Roman Legions coincide with the era of Arthurian Legend. Some believe that Arthur was a Romano-British warrior who fought to hold the land west of the Pennines against foreign invasion, but there is little historical evidence to support this claim. The Legend of the Round Table might as easily have been enacted in Wales or south-west England. But, as later generations of artists and writers have demonstrated, it is hard to imagine a more perfect setting than the Lake District for this great mediaeval romance. Scott based his Arthurian novel 'Bridal of Triermain' at St. John's-in-the-Vale, and Tennyson drew inspiration for passages of his 'Morte D'Arthur' from the Lake District.

king arthur

We do know that in the sixth century Anglian peoples from Germany arrived on the Northumbrian coast. The power of the Celtic (or British) kingdoms was in decline and, after a struggle, the Anglian invaders triumphed over them.

These were agricultural people, not sheep farmers, and they settled in the most fertile parts of Cumbria. Meanwhile the native tribes, among them perhaps the descendants of the legendary Arthur, were forced to continue their farming and herding of sheep on the higher, poorer land.

Langdale Pikes

Maiden Holme and Crowe Holme, Windermere

Skiddaw

Lake Windermere
The Screes, Wast Water *opposite*

About two hundred years after the Anglians there came another invasion, this time of Scandinavian origin. The Norse settlers did not arrive in force but gradually infiltrated Cumbria from the west, moving their sheep and other livestock to the remote, wooded valleys which even the native Britons had not penetrated. These were third or fourth generation Vikings who had already assimilated elements of Gaelic culture into their own, having arrived in northern England from Ireland and the Isle of Man. This fusion of cultures is demonstrated in the great carved stone crosses, decorated with a mixture of Christian and pagan symbols, which they erected throughout the land.

The Norsemen

As they travelled inland the Norsemen named the undiscovered lakes and mountains in the language of their homelands—the words 'tarn', 'dale', 'beck', and 'fell', for example, can all be found on modern maps of Norway. Their method of settling the land followed the Scandinavian pattern too. A farm would be built at the entrance to a dale, and a clearing, or 'thwaite', made in the adjoining woodland. The many Cumbrian villages ending in 'thwaite' show just how widespread these settlements were. At first the settlers continued their tradition of moving livestock to summer pastures, and these, in turn, became permanent dwellings and sheep farms. The locations of these summer pastures, or 'shielings', are indicated by the endings 'erg' or 'er' (from the Gaelic), or by 'saeter' (or 'seat', 'side'). Thus Mosser was 'the shieling on the moss', Seatoller 'the saeter among alder trees', and Ambleside 'Amal's shieling'.

Pigs were kept in the woods, and these places can also

Derwent Water and
Long Side, Skiddaw

be identified by their names. Swindale comes from 'svina' meaning swine, and Grizedale and Grasmere from 'griss', Scandinavian for pig. The names of the mountains too are often derived from the Norse tongue—Scafell and High Scawdel come from the word 'skalli', meaning bald; Crinkle Crags, which encircle the head of Great Langdale, from 'kringla', a circle. Even the speech of the Scandinavians has left its impression on the Cumbrian dialect, giving it what Norman Nicholson, a well-known contemporary writer on the Lakes, has called its 'harshly melodious tune'. The sport of Cumberland wrestling owes a debt to the Vikings, who are said to have introduced it to the region. Even Wordsworth, the great poet of the Lakes, came from Norse stock.

Silver Crag and
Patterdale Common

Woods near Grasmere

Ullswater and Glencoynedale
Crummock Water *opposite*

New Hutton, Heversham and Morecambe Bay

Windermere from near Troutbeck

The tenth and eleventh centuries were times of upheaval and inter-tribal wars, and even the momentous events of 1066 had no immediate impact on Cumbria. The Domesday Survey, completed twenty years after the Norman Conquest, makes no mention of the area; but by the end of the century the Norman barons had marched north and taken control.

Here, as was their custom, they not only built castles but founded monasteries. Priories were situated at Carlisle, St. Bee's, Barrow-in-Furness, and elsewhere; and these were to play a significant part in Cumbria's development. The red sandstone remains of Furness Abbey still give an indication of Norman power and influence.

The Norman Conqvest

The monks were great agriculturalists and did much to improve the land. By 1200 Furness Abbey alone had brought two thousand acres of arable land into cultivation, draining the valleys and clearing tracts of forest. As the population increased the demand for land resulted in ever larger areas being cleared until only the central fells remained untouched. The monasteries rapidly became the largest land-owners, and the new prosperity led to the growth of market towns at Penrith, Ravenglass, and Kendal. For about three hundred years the monks controlled the economy of much of the Lake District.

After the Battle of Bannockburn the Scots began a series of sorties into Cumbria. These continued throughout the fourteenth century, with the wealthier towns in particular suffering at the hands of the raiders. The many stone towers and fortified houses which can still be seen are a legacy from these days.

When, in the 1530's, the monasteries were dissolved and their lands sold off by the Crown, trade which had been routed through the Church now increased the wealth of the market towns. But, more importantly, a new independence, a freedom from outside influences, came to Cumbria.

Mickleden and Rossett Gill, Langdale

Drystone Wall and Copper Beech
Hopegill Head *opposite*

Two Cats, Langdale

The Honey Pot Shop, Hawkshead

Grange Crags, Borrowdale
Derwent Water and Bassenthwaite *opposite*

Summer visitors to the Lakes rarely appreciate the severity of the climate during the long winter months. Life, to the farming folk of the sixteenth and seventeenth centuries, was by no means as idyllic as it may appear to us nowadays.

Farm equipment was still primitive: ploughs, of a type introduced by the Anglians, were heavy and cumbersome; and sledges, rather than carts provided transport over the steep terrain. Longer journeys depended on the use of pack-horses and the early transport routes can still be traced by the many stone pack-horse bridges which remain.

Oats, barley, and beans were among the staple crops grown on the small farms. Oats were particularly important as a large part of the diet consisted of porridge and oatcakes (or 'clap-bread', as the oatcakes were known). No root crops were grown and this made it difficult to keep livestock over the winter. With the exception of a few cows and oxen, most animals were slaughtered in the autumn and the salted meat hung in the open chimneys to dry.

Pack-Horses and Herdwicks

Sheep were, and still are, the mainstay of the farm economy. These were an early type of Herdwick—a sturdy breed which may have been introduced by the Neolithic herdsmen; although a more romantic theory suggests that the first Herdwicks were washed ashore from a shipwrecked Spanish galleon at the time of the Armada. Initially the word 'herdwick' referred to the pasture where the sheep were kept.

Many years ago the villagers of Wasdalehead recognised the Herdwick's canny instinct for survival when they noticed how the flock would ascend the mountain into a threatening snowstorm to avoid being caught in drifts on the sheltered side. It became a local law that no-one should sell more than five ewes per year, in order to keep the breed in the village. More recently, Beatrix Potter, who came to live and farm in the Lake District, became a recognised authority on Herdwicks and often judged the sheep at local shows. Nowadays other, finer woolled breeds have been introduced, but the Herdwicks are still numerous and remain a common sight on the fells.

Kendal's motto is 'Pannus Mihi Panis'—wool is my bread—and the coarse woollen cloth known as 'Kendal Cottons' was a mainstay of the rural economy for many years. The cloth was manufactured in the dales as part of a cottage industry. Kendal was also a market place for the mineral wealth of the fells. Slate, lead, silver, and copper were quarried and mined; but, by the

beginning of the eighteenth century, mining, like the wool trade, was in decline.

Yet, although the sound of the coppersmiths' hammers was no longer heard in the streets of the market towns, the activities of the Mines Royal had made a lasting impression on the countryside. The demand for charcoal, used in smelting and the manufacture of crude iron, led to the destruction of much of the deciduous forest. Other woodland crafts, such as the making of barrels and matting, also contributed to the process of deforestation.

The earliest settlers had encountered a landscape where all but the highest mountains had been covered in oak, birch, and pine forest rising from valleys of unmanageable swampland. By the end of the eighteenth century, when the Agrarian Revolution finally reached the wilds of Cumbria, that primeval terrain had already been dramatically altered.

Tilberthwaite Fells

Great Langdale Beck *opposite*

Grange, Borrowdale

Great Gable and Upper Borrowdale

In 1790 a correspondent of the Gentleman's Magazine wrote of south Cumberland, 'The rust of poverty and ignorance is gradually wearing off . . . the houses (or rather huts) of clay, which were small and ill-built, are mostly thrown down; instead of which strong and roomy farmhouses are built . . . with hard, durable stone, which is very plentiful here'. No one can visit the Lake District without noticing the distinctive use of stone as a building material. Most of these new farmhouses were built by the more prosperous dalesmen and, when complete, they were roughcast then whitewashed. Many of these houses still exist, but it is interesting to note that Wordsworth objected to them— on the grounds that the white-washed buildings were too conspicuous and detracted from the beauty of the dales. Perhaps in unconscious sympathy with the poet's wishes the more recent trend in building has been to leave the stone untouched.

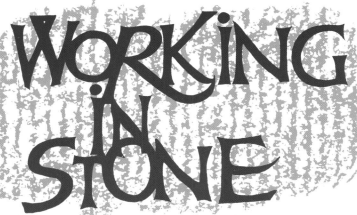

WORKING IN STONE

One final feature was added to the landscape as we know it today— parts of the fells were enclosed with drystone dykes, as a way of making the management of sheep easier. The skills involved in building the dykes have never been lost and most modern farmers still maintain the dykes in preference to other forms of fencing.

The difficulties experienced in moving troops through Cumberland during the 1745 rebellion emphasised the need for better roads. Soon a road was built from Newcastle to Carlisle, and others followed. The introduction of a carrier-wagon service between London and Kendal heralded the end of the pack-horse in all but the remote dales. Yet while many Cumbrian towns became important coaching centres, the western dales and central mountains remained virtually unknown. The valleys of western Lakeland were not even mapped until the 1770's and, as late as 1801, Dorothy Wordsworth, living in Grasmere, thought it worthy of note that, 'today a chaise passed'. It would not be long, however, before the chaise, the stage-coach, and even the locomotive, arrived in numbers— bringing with them the first eager tourists.

Eskdale
Borrowdale *previous page*

Black Lamb and Mother

Base Brown and Grange Crags

Buttermere
Rough Holme and Thomson's Holme, Windermere *opposite*

High Rigg and Great Dodd
Little Langdale and Bow Fell *opposite*

Kentmere
Barn Door *opposite*
High Rigg, Calfhow Pike and Great Dodd *next page*

Ullswater near Pooley Bridge
Whiteside End, Kentmere *opposite*

High Scawdel, Borrowdale
Latterbarrow and Windermere *opposite*

River Derwent and Derwent Water

Eskdale Post Office

A few early travellers had passed through the Lake District in search of antiquities, or local curiosities, but it was not until late in the eighteenth century that the dales-folk realised they had more than archaeological remains and quaint folk tales to offer visitors. They had 'the picturesque'.

In 1767 a 'Description of the Lake and Vale of Keswick' by a Dr John Brown was published. Shortly after this the poet Thomas Gray made a tour of the Lakes and wrote enthusiastically about this little known part of England. Well-to-do southerners followed in his footsteps and the 'Tour' of Lakeland became a fashionable alternative to the 'Grand Tour' of Europe.

The term 'picturesque' was coined by William Gilpin, a schoolmaster from Surrey. His own 'Lakes Tour' of 1786 was a best-seller which did more than any other account to popularise the region. As the leading authority on the picturesque—by which he meant scenery which was not merely beautiful but contained an element of wild disarray—he

The Picturesque

established a cult which attracted scores of sightseers to the Lakes. 'The pleasures of the chase are universal', mused Gilpin, 'and shall we suppose it a greater pleasure to the sportsman to pursue a trivial animal, than it is for the man of taste to pursue the beauties of nature?' But not everyone took the schoolmaster's ideas with the seriousness he intended. A contemporary parody begins with the lines:

"Your sport, my Lord, I cannot take,
For I must go and hunt a lake;
And while you chase the flying deer,
I must fly off to Windermere . . ."

White Moss and
Grasmere

Coniston Water

Little Loughrigg, near Ambleside

The native Cumbrians, for so long accustomed to a meagre diet of porridge and cheese, must have viewed the growing tourist trade with incredulity. Still, they were not slow to exploit its potential.

Maps and guidebooks appeared, conducting visitors to selected viewpoints and places of interest; inns sprang up along the tourist routes; regattas were introduced onto the lakes; and hotels began to keep small fleets of boats for hire. Most of the inns, and some of the boats, were equipped with cannons which, for the fee of a few shillings, would send an echo rolling round the hills. At times musicians would be taken in the boats to provide appropriate 'water-music' as the scene unfolded. Locals would be hired as guides and as bearers of the enormous picnic hampers with which the sightseers fortified themselves for the pursuit of the picturesque.

About this time too it became fashionable to build large gothic-style houses on the banks of the lakes. Wray Castle, on the shores of Windermere, is a well-known example.

Inns emerged in the more remote dales—at Buttermere, Rosthwaite, Ennerdale, and Borrowdale—and eventually the railways came, providing the final impetus needed to establish the Lake District as England's foremost tourist centre.

The first railway, to Windermere via Kendal, was built in the late 1840's and was intended to promote trade. It was meant to continue as far as Ambleside but local pressure, exerted by Wordsworth among others, stopped its progress at the tiny village of Birthwaite. Here the town of Windermere grew—a rarity among Lake towns in that, architecturally, it is almost entirely of the nineteenth century.

Cannons and Water-Music

Derwent Water, Cat Bells and Crag Hill

Fairfield *opposite*

River Esk

Colthouse Heights and Windermere

Great Langdale and The Band

If the early tourists were in search of the picturesque, a new generation was drawn by something rather different. William Wordsworth, the leading poet of the Romantic movement, was a native Cumbrian who spent most of his life in the heart of the Lake District. His reputation, and his celebration of the Lakes in verse, made the area a centre of pilgrimage for the intelligentsia of the nineteenth century.

Wordsworth and his sister Dorothy, whose diaries of these eventful years have become a literary classic in their own right, were born in Cockermouth. Most of William's education took place at Hawkshead Grammar School, and after time spent at Cambridge University and travelling in Europe, he settled with his sister in Grasmere. Here they were joined by Mary Hutchinson, whom Wordsworth married in 1802. Dove Cottage, their first home in Grasmere, has been carefully preserved and stands next to a Wordsworth museum. It was in this cottage that the poet composed some of his finest works, among them 'Michael', 'Intimations of Immortality', and 'The Prelude'. Later the family left Grasmere and moved the short distance south to Rydal Mount. This house is also open to the public and the garden has been reconstructed as Wordsworth himself created it. The family grave is in the local churchyard in Grasmere.

Much of Wordsworth's poetry is woven around his experiences in the Lake District—both as a child and as an adult—and the solitude and natural beauty he found there are essential ingredients in his work. Nature meant more to him than the picturesque or the beautiful; it was the moving spirit of the world which could mirror our deepest thoughts and

Wordsworth and the Lake Poets

Thornythwaite Fell and Scafell Pikes

feelings, and raise us to new levels of experience:

> "To him was given an ear which deeply felt
> The voice of Nature in the obscure wind
> The sounding mountain and the running stream."

All around Grasmere and Rydal Mount are the forest walks, the lake and mountain scenery, which the poet loved so much. He wrote too of the country folk, the beggars and the shepherds; often drawing from their simple lives the same deep truths that he found in Nature itself. One wonders what they thought of Wordsworth as he wandered to and fro, lonely as the proverbial cloud, composing his verses aloud or standing 'rapt in philosophical speculation' in front of some ruined cottage.

Wordsworth was a recluse and did little to encourage admirers, always preferring the solitude of the fells, or the company of a few close friends to that of society at large. Among these friends were the poets Samuel Taylor Coleridge and Robert Southey, both of whom came to live in the Lake District. Along with Wordsworth they formed the nucleus of the 'Lake Poets'. Both Shelley and Keats visited the Lakes and, by association, were included in the group. Thomas De Quincey, a would-be disciple of Wordsworth, came north as a young man and was a frequent visitor for the rest of his life. He married a local girl and lived for a time in Wordsworth's old home, Dove Cottage.

The sundial above the front door of Wordsworth's old school in Hawkshead

His book 'Recollections of the Lakes and the Lake Poets' is justly famous for the insights it gives into both the Wordsworth circle and rural society at the time.

Other great figures visited what had come to be known as 'Wordsworth country', among them Charles Lamb, William Hazlitt, and Sir Walter Scott. Scott and Wordsworth climbed Helvellyn together, each composing a poem to celebrate the occasion. In later life the art critic John Ruskin settled near Coniston Water and the great Victorian poets Tennyson and Mathew Arnold also spent time among the Lakes. Arnold lived at Under Loughrigg and became an enthusiastic fell-walker—a pursuit which the Lake Poets had done much to popularise.

In fact fell-walking was a fairly recent past-time. Its introduction is credited to a Captain Joseph Budworth, a colourful character who arrived in the Lake District in the 1790's. Despite having only one arm this redoubtable gentleman conquered Skiddaw, Helvellyn, Coniston Old Man, Helm Crags, and the Langdale Pikes. These ascents probably did much to allay the fears felt by early tourists who were unused to such awesome scenery. Christopher North, the Scots poet and philosopher, was another pioneer of fell-walking—as well as being an avid boxer, wrestler, and horseman. Nowadays fell-walking is probably the most popular pursuit among visitors to the Lakes. Credit for this is due not only to Budworth and the poets but, more recently, to Alfred Wainwright whose books on the subject have introduced thousands to the mountains of Cumbria.

Nether How, near Buttermere *next page*

Not a breath of air
Ruffles the bosom of this leafy glen.
From the brook's margin, wide around, the trees
Are steadfast as the rocks; the brook itself,
Old as the hills that feed it from afar,
Doth rather deepen than disturb the calm
Where all things else are still and motionless.

William Wordsworth.

Grasmere *opposite*

Nab Cottage, by Rydal Water
Red Bank, Grasmere *opposite*

'Hill Top', near Sawrey—Beatrix Potter's Cottage

The Tower Bank Arms, near Sawrey—featured in *'The Tale of Jemima Puddleduck'*

The literary connection with the Lakes has continued into the present century. Beatrix Potter, creator of Peter Rabbit and Squirrel Nutkin, may be far removed from Wordsworth or Coleridge but she gained inspiration from the same surroundings. Her homes at Hill Top Cottage near Sawrey, and Lingholm on the shore of Derwent Water rival Dove Cottage and Rydal Mount as tourist attractions, and those familiar with her tales explore the nearby woods and villages in search of the original settings.

THE

LAKES

Arthur Ransome, another childrens' favourite, based his 'Swallows and Amazons' around Coniston Water and

IN THE TWENTIETH CENTURY

Windermere; and Hugh Walpole's historical romances take place in Borrowdale. Walpole's novels portray the countryside and customs of the region with great accuracy. Judith Paris, one of his heroines, reputedly lived in Watendlath—an isolated cluster of stone buildings looking onto a hill-top tarn and flanked by an ancient pack-horse bridge. In such places the visitor is transported back in time, and the inspirational qualities which writers, artists, and photographers still find in the landscape of the Lake District become obvious.

Appropriately it was Wordsworth who first envisaged the region as a 'sort of national property' and, in a sense, his dream has been realised. Within the Lake District National Park, as most of central Lakeland is now known, the National Trust owns over 125,000 acres.

Already the Trust has done much good work, both in preserving historic buildings and sites and protecting the ecology of the land. But the district must accommodate many interests besides those of the tourists and conservationists.

Many thousands of people work in the region—farmers, reservoir workers, craftsmen, shop-keepers, and quarrymen—and while sheep have remained at the heart of the economy

Watendlath Tarn

forestry has become increasingly important. The Forestry Commission has, however, adopted policies which are aimed at conserving this unique landscape. They have agreed not to purchase land in the central fells, allowing them to remain open country, and they have avoided some of the regimentation and ecological hazards associated with quick-growing conifers by planting deciduous trees as well. These methods have helped to preserve the region's wildlife and flora.

Red squirrels, roe deer, golden eagles, ravens, and peregrine falcons are among the many, often rare, species to be found in Cumbria. Increasingly, the ranks of fell-walkers, mountaineers, windsurfers, and sightseers have been joined by botanists and naturalists. The delicate alpine flowers found in the high fells, the unusual species of fish found in the lakes (survivors of the last Ice Age), the oak woods ringing with birdsong, the bluebells and primroses in the meadows—these have all survived the changing centuries. With our continued consideration and help they will survive for many more.

Ullswater and
Gowbarrow Fell

High Scawdel, Borrowdale

Derwent Water

Rain, Grange, Borrowdale

The Britannia, Elterwater
Great Langdale *opposite*

Frosty Morning, Lake Windermere

List of Plates